THE INTELLECTUAL BONDAGE OF OUR CHILDREN

DON'T BLAME THE TEACHERS
BLAME THE SYSTEM

BY KENT SWANSON

© 2009 Kent Swanson

All Rights Reserved

No part of this book may be reproduced in any form or by any means without permission in writing from the publisher, Greentimber Schoolhouse P.O. Box 787 Ashton, Idaho 83420

ISBN 978-0-97823749-0-0

Contents

Introduction..1

The Natural Learning Process..3

Every Child Has the Right to Their Own Intellectual Destiny.....7

The Brain Hole..11

The Power of Observation, Inspiration and Practical Experience.............13

Vantage Point..15

Our Presentation...17

A Walk Down Memory Lane...19

A Teacher..23

Fast Absorbers..25

Blueprint...27

The Negative Unintended Consequences.................................29

Home-schooling: a Poor Choice? 31

The Immature Brain...35

The Mature Brain...37

Primary and Secondary Interest and Information....................39

Internal Motivation……………………………………..………...…41

Positive Reinforcement…………………………………...……43

Daydreaming………………………………………………..….45

Trial and Error……………………………………………….....47

Physical Activity and Learning…………...……………………49

Learning by Observing………………………………………...51

Be Happy……………………………………………………....53

Social Skills…………………………………………………....55

The Kid Culture………………………………………..………57

The Value of a Community………………………………..…..59

For Your Information…..……………………………………...61

Oppression and Discrimination…...…………………………...63

Learning Is a Process, Not a System…...……………………...65

Little Things are Big Things…………………………………..67

Leaving the "You Got To" Syndrome…………………….…...69

Passive Entertainment and the Unreal World……………….…71

Qualities of a Person……………………………………………..………......73

A Formula for Success……………………………………………..………....75

Analogies………………………………………………………………..………...77

I Can Only Imagine……………………………………………………..……...91

Research and Development…………………………………………….…...97

The Jelling and Healing Affects of a Family Learning Together……….99

Children Are Our Future………………………………………..………....101

In the Future……………………………………………………………..……...103

The Future Vacation…………………………………………………..….....105

What is the Human Experience? …………………..……………….......107

A Change Will Do You Good……………………………………….……...109

Options…….…………………………………………………………….……...111

The Truth is Hidden or We Would Not Be Able to Find It………..…..113

The Ostrich Effect………………………………………………….…..…....115

Ingenuity……………………………………………………..……..………...117

From the Author………………………………………………..………...119

Order Form…………………………………………………………..……...122

iii

Introduction

Our children have an incredible capacity for learning. A child's brain is more complicated and advanced than any computer we will ever build. So why does it take 13 years for our current school system to implant such simple tasks into our children's brains? It is amazing the amount of resources we invest in the current system for the limited results we achieve.

There is no doubt in my mind that our intentions are good, heartfelt and seemingly boundless; but it appears that this effort, no matter how much we increase it, will not achieve anything greater than it has already achieved. We have, in effect by its design, trapped our children's intelligence in a dysfunctional world of paranoia and sterility. The chains that bind our children are forged link by link from our lack of faith in our children's natural ability to learn.

A child's life begins in the arms of his or her parents. Parents watch their children in short order, without much help, learn to effectively move their muscles to achieve mastery of their bodies and learn to speak a language all in a very short period of time. As their child progresses, parents see something else, something indescribable: a potential to achieve something unique to the child, as if they were sent here for a purpose. It's as if the knowledge is already there and just needs time to mature. They see a child full of curiosity and fascination. They see a child full of motivation to understand the world around them.

It is not uncommon for parents to abandon these early observations after our children have been in school. Adjusting our expectations to a new reality and accepting the assessment of our school system as a hard dose of reality.

What if all children have an unlimited capacity to learn and enrich our lives? What if the school system we created to nurture our children has become an intellectual prison? What if the system is preventing our children from achieving their potential by the way we structured it? That would mean that we are spending a lot of money on the problem instead of the solution. I know this is a bold statement, but I do not think anyone would disagree that our school system has problems.

Our children are too precious to accept the results we currently achieve. A lot of thought and effort has gone into evaluating ways to improve our current school system. Is it possible that the mere structure of the school system is the problem and the solution is creating a new system that enables the natural learning process already hard-wired inside all children?

The Natural Learning Process

What is the natural learning process? The natural learning process is the interfacing of an individual and the dynamics of life through the numerous hard-wired natural learning pathways and processes in the brain. If the human brain would have evolved in a school environment it would be better suited to perform in that environment. The human brain did not; it evolved in the real world of complex sensory input. The brain evolved to intuitively engage with life, it evolved with the ability to fill in gaps in information, to draw from inspiration, to create and test theories, to apply knowledge from one experience to another similar experience and it evolved with an intense desire to understand the natural world around it. By taking the brain out of its natural learning environment we have disabled it and created nonexistent learning disabilities. Throughout this book, you will see references to the natural learning process. Obviously children learn naturally, but that learning ability is designed to function in a different environment than we currently provide for them in school. This book tries to point out why our school system inhibits the potential of our children to learn by contrasting this simple observation with the current process we have employed to help our children learn.

A natural learning environment legitimizes the individual by providing for and the respecting of a child's right to their own intellectual destiny and challenges the brain processes that were developed by the natural world. The natural learning process is powerful. In my experiences I have only scratched the surfaces and have seen the empowering effects of allowing our children to develop their unique talents, skills and internal motivation.

The natural learning process enables a child to find his or her own path in life. Since we are all unique individuals, this process is important not only to our success, but to our happiness. If we cannot express our individuality we cannot determine the purpose of our life.

Not only is the natural learning process more effective, it sustains the soul of a child. The natural learning process is a complete food for a child's brain so to speak. I believe if we were to provide a natural learning environment for our children we would see most, if not all, of the barriers to learning go away. A lot of our time and resources go to assessing how our children are doing. We have developed a sophisticated and intelligent process for this. Might this system become obsolete if we convert our schools to a natural learning environment? I think it will.

Every Child has the Right to Their Own Intellectual Destiny

There is a fundamental guiding principal that should be applied when establishing a new learning system: choice, and the right of a child to choose how, what, when and where knowledge is obtained and the right not to be graded, tested, sorted or evaluated by an external entity for the purpose of applying narrow quantitative assessment. The assessment of a child should be a choice, made by the child and it should be made clear that the assessment is for establishing a marker relevant to the purposes set by the child. A child's right to choose eliminates the need to stand in front of a class, dictate information and then test to see how much was absorbed. We have to get past the idea that we know what our children need to know to succeed in life. The simple skills we now try to implant in our children, can simply attach themselves to the internally motivated paths children lay out for themselves.

A new incentive for a school system should be to create a more natural learning environment that will allow a child the opportunity to selectively learn, follow their curiosity, play, pretend, explore and develop without being put into a category.

I cannot help but wonder how many gifted children have been oppressed in the developmental stages of learning by preconceived ideas of success or intellectual evaluations that stereotype children. How have we affected society by disabling children's natural and unique intelligence? We have to stop thinking that children's brains are empty vessels. We have to stop applying monetary gain to the process of learning as a definition for success.

Absorption rate is the current system's measure of intelligence. What an arrogant, premature and narrow criteria for determining intelligence and advancement. In order to illustrate the flaw in this way of thinking I like to use this example, a child receives a test score of 50%. In most schools this would warrant a poor grade. The 50% right proves that, given enough time, the child would learn the other 50%. The fact is the child is absorbing the information. Giving the children back the right to their own intellectual destiny will eliminate a fundamental mistake our current system has inflicted on our children.

In our society, the fast absorbers are considered to be more intelligent than slow absorbers. To make the situation worse, our school system starts making the absorption rate assessments at such a young age, at a time when a child should be freely expressing their own intellectual destiny. I am concerned that the absorption rate assessments can become an enabler to the children that achieve this status and provides another reason to create an oppressive social order. A child's absorption rate is affected by external and internal factors controlled by the learning environment as well as by the age of the child. We should not measure the absorption rate; we should be actively promoting its enlargement in children

Visualize an opening into the brain. It dilates and constricts based on internal and external factors. Absorption rate is controlled by this opening. Measuring it in some children merely reduces its size. Instead, we should be actively pursuing activities that open it to its maximum size in all children. Pushing more information than can pass through the opening just closes it even more. Choice is the fertile ground for curiosity, fascination, motivation and inspiration- all dilators of a child's brain hole.

Choice, a huge brain opening dilator provides for a phenomenon that is not legitimized by our current system, a phenomenon that has contributed a lot to mankind. I like to call this phenomenon "intellectual soup." Choice enables a child to put together knowledge from unrelated disciplines, creating great contributions to society.

The Brain Hole

The brain hole, I have never seen it but I know it exists. It is the opening into the brain that controls what type and how fast information flows in. They vary in size and shape for each child. The size controls the speed and the shape controls the type of information. At any given moment the size and shape can change in a child. If learning becomes a job, if information is forced in too fast, if a child's confidence is tampered with the brain hole closes. If curiosity, fascination, choice or play is injected into a learning environment, the brain hole stretches to open as big as it can. You have probably experienced the effects of this opening even as an adult.

The brain hole concept makes the current school system obsolete. Too much of the school environment constricts the brain hole. The brain hole does not stay open all the time. Quite often, it closes to digest and stir the information around inside. The brain hole can be readily opened from outside stimulation but when it closes it is important we leave it alone. The brain hole can be very selective. A little bit of this a little bit of that. There might be an obvious direction to a child's curiosity or it might be random.

The brain hole is connected to a part of the brain that defines our essence, our individuality, our personality and our internal motivation. When we measure what is considered a child's intelligence in effect we are trying to measure the brain hole. You can see the futility in this. When it is open it might not be learning what you plan to teach it. It may have absorbed the information but the storing process makes it hard to retrieve. The selectivity of the hole might only let in a percentage of the information. What we want a child to learn may not be what a child wants to learn.

Legitimize the brain hole and you legitimize the natural learning process. It is impossible to measure intelligence. It is infinite in scope. It is directly influenced by external forces. It is not a limitation. It is a mystery ready to unfold.

The Power of Observation, Inspiration and Practical Experience

The experts are not going to solve our education problems. They have had enough time to solve the problems. They would have done it by now if they could. We have to draw from our experience as students and as parents of students to create a system that enhances the natural learning process not suppresses it. We have to create a system that is molded around the child not a system that requires a child to mold around it.

It is easy to be intimidated by such a huge educational system, but the fact is, the learning process is simple and everyone does it. You might not have a firm grasp of the content of knowledge, but you know what environment you learn best in. That legitimizes you to have an opinion about what kind of system your child should be in.

It has been my experience that children do not like to be sorted, categorized and judged. They do not like it when learning becomes a job. Children thrive in an environment of fascination, challenge, curiosity and play.

There is no substitute for the powers of observation, inspiration and practical experience. Typically the only thing missing for an individual to act upon these observations is confidence. Confidence might be a luxury we don't have. We have to be driven to create a better system out of the concern for our children's well being even if we don't have that confidence.

It is understandable that people would go to great lengths to make the current system work. We have invested a lot of money in it, people's livelihoods depend on it, and a different system brings the unknown.

Our children deserve a system better than the one we have now. Where do we start? The good news is we do not have to start from scratch. We have the infrastructure, we have personnel and we have capitol. This does not need to get complicated. Parents have spent 13 years experiencing the system and 13 years experiencing the system through their children. This combined 26 years qualifies them to make observations.

Basic observations will be the most critical elements in creating a new system. The following are some observations I have made watching our children. You may have made other observations watching your own children. These observations are invaluable. Use them, embrace them, they are the most important tools we will have in creating the school system of the future.

Vantage Point

Vantage point: A place where just being there gives a person an opportunity to see things no one else can see.

The federal government sees everything from the perspective of money. What is the return on investment in education? Tracking and accountability are the perspective with these goals. Our children are future tax payers; government wants to train them from day one to be productive members of society. What a sterilizing affect this has on society, the irony of this perspective is children do poorly in this type of environment. The potential for a child to become a productive member of society actually decreases in this type of environment. Productivity is a function of individuality not conformity.

The school system sees everything from within the parameters of the system as well as from the fact their livelihood depends on the system. Changing the current system creates the fear of the unknown. The options for improving the learning environment within this system are limited.

Parents though they may not have the expertise and have little input in the learning process have the best vantage point for seeing the path our school system should follow. Parents see learning from the point of view of nurturing. Learning in its pure form is nurturing. To nurture a child, parents put their own needs behind their child's. This vantage point is indispensable. Parents are in the best vantage point to understand the natural learning process.

Even though parents have not acted upon their observations they have seen the injustice that is being inflicted on their children. Parents have seen the natural learning potential in their children crushed. Parents have the most to lose if the system is dysfunctional.

You must be a parent to understand this vantage point; there is no other way to get it. We must take advantage of this unique vantage point to develop a new system of educating our children. Parents will be critical in the success of any new school system.

Our Presentation

Have we made school so unappealing that children choose drugs, gangs, sex, etc. over knowledge? I am not blaming these problems on our schools, but can we create a school system that competes better with these intense abuses of life?

There are businesses that can sell anything to us. We respond well to presentation; even food is more appealing when we put effort into the presentation. I think we could remove a lot of the temptation to abuse life by presenting knowledge to our children in a more appealing way. It would be very gratifying to see the intense internal motivation of some children not be used for destructive behavior.

We can't simply accept a reality that some children are bad, and that is just the way it is. Are some children bad or do they just make bad decisions? I can't help but wonder if we have lost some of our great entrepreneurs to drug dealing and some of our great warriors to gangs.

The best weapon we have to combat destructive behavior is respect. In order to get respect from a child, it has to be given to the child, respect for their individuality, their ideas, there unique intellectual path and their self-worth. Respect should be the presentation by which we serve up knowledge to our children. If we show respect to our children, won't they in turn respect themselves, the power of their decisions, other people, knowledge and life.

Investing in our children does not mean throwing money at a school system; it means investing in their ideas and their individuality. We should not just be investing with money, but with our respect, our compassion and our inspiration. The investment should not go to a few children, but to all children.

A Walk Down Memory Lane

Do you remember your school days? What are your earliest memories of school? Do you have fond memories? Are there some bad memories? Did school empower you or did it suppress you? Did school help you find a vocation you would enjoy and were good at or are you just getting by? Did you excel in school or did you struggle? We have all been through the school system, what did we get from it?

We assume it is the foundation of our success. Obviously 13 of those early years spent in school have a profound impact on everyone. How much of what you learned do you still remember? How much of what you learned do you use in your daily life? Did school give you confidence, or did it take your confidence away? When you graduated did you know what you wanted to do with your life? Did you have favorite teachers? Do you remember any bad teachers? Do you feel that you could be an individual in school or did you feel you had to conform?

I remember lying down under a tree after kindergarten thinking how beautiful nature is and how grateful I was to be out of class and wondering why my parents were making me go to school. I remember reading for the first time and realizing other children were doing better than I was. I was the D student that tried hard to rise to the occasion of the C. If I could just get a C, everyone would leave me alone, alone to think about this wonderful world, alone to daydream about adventures. Everything below an A was a degree of failure, this was my impression, but people would accept a C but not a D. Work harder, for what? What was obtaining the knowledge going to do for me? It was not my choice to be there. I was told by my parents that society expects all children to attend and graduate from school.

My school experience was one of obedience. I attended school out of respect for my parents. I put on hold an internal desire to understand what I was all about. Barriers were placed on my self confidence. School gave me a sense of my place in life which controlled my expectations for life. School taught me that the A students would succeed in whatever they pursued. I was glad when school was over, were you?

I am sure a lot of people enjoyed school. The sports, the socializing and the learning opportunities, but did you discover yourself? Did you develop an internal drive to embrace life? Did you develop confidence in yourself? If you enjoyed school did you find life out of school to be like you expected?

I began discovering myself after I got out of school. A skill I had that was not nurtured by school became my life ring. I clung to it out of necessity, it was problem solving. Success became the problem I needed to solve. My school experience did not legitimize a path for me. School would lay out a path for some to succeed but not others. The others, being those who struggled for whatever reason, and could only attain low grades. What about those who got high grades and followed a path laid out by our education system? Are they happy they followed that path?

How did you tackle succeeding in life? How big a role did school play? Did playing sports help your success? Or has a sport injury plagued your health?

Analyzing one's experiences can reveal a wealth of knowledge that can help in charting a new course for our children's future. There is no substitute for experience. Use it wisely, and use it with confidence.

A Teacher

    What a noble profession. A teacher can probably tell you how uplifting and gratifying it is to witness a child learn. They can also tell you how frustrating a classroom can get if learning stops. What happens if learning becomes a job or when learning is trumped by expectations and forced goals? Does a teacher still feel this energizing effect, and, if they do not, what effect does this have on a learning environment? Children are very perceptive, and pick up on frustration.

    I know our teachers have a passion for teaching, and I know the current school system stifles their creativity and talent at every turn, placing a bureaucratic wedge between teachers and the children. This reality has devastating effects on our school system. No longer is there an evolving relationship with children based on inspiration; there is no time for that- just information in and information out. Teachers are doing the best they can with the system we have given them. Administrators are doing the best they can as well with the system we have given them. It is ironic; our ability to see the dysfunction of our school system is cloaked in a noble desire to help our children. I have seen the compassion and concern on administrators' faces when they express their desire for children to get an education. Administrators feel the pressure of the world on their shoulders; they wonder how much longer they can carry the burden by themselves. As they look for solutions to the problems of lower test scores and children losing interest in school we keep adding more pressure on them to perform. It's impossible to fix anything in that type of environment.

Keep our current school system, stifle our teachers and stifle the natural learning process and we can only achieve what we have achieved so far. Our children are in intellectual bondage and so are our teachers because these natural elements of learning are not a part of our public school system. Have faith and enable the natural process of learning and our administrators, teachers and children will benefit. Administrators and teachers need our help; we need to provide them with a learning environment that provides natural learning opportunities between students and teachers. Teachers did not choose their careers to be slaves to a huge bureaucracy. The magic of learning between a student and a teacher needs to be rediscovered. A teacher, without that positive reinforcement, will die inside; the money is not why they teach.

A natural learning environment would make a teacher feel more like a conductor of an orchestra instead of a drill sergeant in the army.

Fast Absorbers

Our current school system does not meet the needs of our F, D and C students, but does it provide a fertile environment for our A and B students? That is the irony of our current situation. The fast absorbers typically feel held back by our system. I believe it is for the same reason children struggle in our current system. There are no intellectual freedoms.

Fast absorbers want to follow an intellectual path only to find they need to do tasks that hold them back or slow them down. Shooting for the middle of a target leaves the rest of the target untouched. There is no way for our current school system to provide an education for everyone.

Children are so varied in their learning predispositions that the only way to provide for all of them is allowing them to follow their own natural path. The natural path to learning allows each child to expand on their strong points, develop strengths in weaknesses, tie knowledge to the real world, develop internal motivation and develop techniques for learning in the real world, all behavior that will evolve naturally.

Children are designed to learn in a natural environment. They are not designed to learn in a man-made learning system that does not give credence to the natural learning processes. Like the slow absorbers, the fast absorbers become handicapped in our current system as well. Ironically, the current school system likes to point to their success with fast absorbers as justification for their existence. The reality is that their successes are actually not successes at all.

Blueprint

Our school system is a blueprint for our society. How we go about providing education directly affects our society. Is the blueprint of our current system designed to insure we become productive members of society? When we place monetary gain as the fundamental reason for an education, we should not be surprised when people place monetary gain above humanity.

The sports in school teach there are winners and losers. To succeed in this blueprint someone must win and someone must lose; survival of the fittest. Only the children that test high can go on in the education world to attain lucrative jobs. We will not remove primitive and distasteful behavior from our society, but we do not have to encourage it. Win/lose or win/win, survival of the fittest or stretching a helping hand down. Test, sort and pick out the winners of an intellectual game or provide a stimulating environment for learning to all.

There are profound differences in results between these approaches. It is not a surprise that our school system embraces and facilitates the fast absorbers. These fast absorbers will gain momentum over the slow absorbers and eventually win in the game created by the current system. It is understandable that the current system does not want to waste resources on children that are losing. Is this the blueprint we want for our society?

In this current school system, where do we legitimize entrepreneurial thinking, where do we legitimize inspiration, where do we legitimize individuality, morality and compassion? These are critical building blocks for society.

How often do we lure some of our fast absorbers into professional pursuits, only to find out that they prefer to be a mom, a farmer or just something simpler? Happiness can only be defined by the individual, not by monetary gain or the system.

I cannot help but wonder if we have lost some of our most gifted students, because we did not recognize or legitimize their potential because of their absorption speed. A passion-driven person can tap the most powerful sources of knowledge (inspiration). Without inspiration, mankind would still be in the Stone Age.

What a sterile environment the pursuit of monetary gain creates. Give our children back their individuality, their freedom to choose and their right to their own intellectual destiny. I would like to see how that blueprint would bless society and the children in it.

The Negative Unintended Consequences

The effort of our society to educate our children has been a noble one. Over the years we have spared no expense. It is not uncommon for a noble effort to have opposite and unintended consequences. Declining test scores, apathy, a lack of enthusiasm, depression, violence and the need to medicate to conform to the learning environment are a few of the negative unintended consequences.

The school system did not intend to create the problems we face in school. The goal of all schools is to give our children the knowledge they need to succeed in life. When negative unintended consequences occur the tendency is to accept them if the benefits outweigh the negatives. When police officers have to be in our schools, children have to be drugged to conform to our school system and children bring guns to school and kill students and faculty, then it's time to reevaluate the system. These negative consequences are not natural; they exist because of the structure of the system our children are in.

Do not look for the honest reevaluation to come from within the school system. When people's livelihoods are at stake, objectivity is lost. Problem solving is confined by the parameters of a system that is too narrow.

Negative unintended consequences happen when we don't totally understand something. With all the years of practice and all the scientific analysis, it is hard to accept the possibility that we do not understand the learning process. The proof that we do not understand the learning process is the results we receive. The proof lies in the anger and frustration in the individuals sighting the need for more money to improve the results of our school systems. The proof lies in the obsession of endless testing and categorizing of children that accomplish nothing accept intimidation.

I have to wonder even though it appears we do not understand the learning process that maybe we have just forgotten it. Maybe we have betrayed the human experience of learning by injecting our arrogance and lack of faith in the natural learning process.

Negative unintended consequences in a learning environment should be the trigger for the reevaluation of a system. Negativity never motivates, it just intimidates. The negative behavior we see in our children in school is their intellect rebelling against an oppressive and sterile learning environment. The negative behavior will only get worse as time passes. The negative behavior is not manageable. If we do not take a step back and consider the natural learning process as a legitimate system, the negative unintended consequences will eventually collapse the current school system and at what cost to our children and society?

Home-Schooling: A Poor Choice?

My wife and I started our first three children in the public school system. Things went well for about three years then an adversarial relationship began to develop between the school and our family. The situation deteriorated to the point that we began looking into home-schooling our children. The responsibilities seemed too great, but the alternative compromised our responsibilities as parents.

After we began home-schooling I was overwhelmed by the number of parents who came up to me and asked how home-school was going. They quickly remarked that they had considered home-schooling their children, but felt overwhelmed or were concerned with their child's social skills and decided not to. It is so common to this day that I have to believe, even though I have no concrete data, over 50% of parents have given thought to home-schooling. This is a modern day phenomenon. What causes this response in parents? What causes the resentment by some people when parents choose to home-school? Why do home-school children do so well? If you research these questions you will find a wealth of knowledge.

The choice to home-school is difficult to explain. It is not a statement directed at the Teachers or administration. It is a leap of faith. The fact is home-schooling is a poor choice. Most home-schoolers have fewer resources than the public school system. Parents have a limited amount of time to invest in home schooling. The choice is made because the parent sees no other option.

After the choice is made, there is a time when parents try to emulate the public school system. This can be a time of frustration and doubt. Some parents maintain a similar system to the public school. Other parents systems evolve into something unique to their family.

Even though home-school families teach differently, there are common threads passing through all of them. Those threads are what produce the successes in home-schools. They are simple yet profound. They are missing from our public school system. Simply put them in and our public school system would flourish. Home-school families simply tapped the natural learning environment of intellectual freedom. No need for vouchers and no need to keep increasing revenue to solve the problems. No need for government intervention like no child left behind.

Home-schoolers have something to teach the public school system. Animosity and arrogance are the only things standing in the way. How else do you explain the lack of interest in the forces behind the successes home-schoolers achieve? Home-schooling is not the ideal answer however; I know there is an enormous amount of creative ideas for ways to improve our children's learning environment. By the time a home-schooling family figures out a beneficial technique their child may not be able to benefit from it. Creating a school system where we can gather our successful ideas together and provide them to all children in a public school is the logical approach.

The Immature Brain

There are two types of brain realities: the immature brain and the mature brain. The immature brain thrives in a different environment than the mature brain.

The worst thing you can do to an immature brain is assess it based on a narrow and rudimentary interpretation of knowledge. Believe it or not, the immature brain is more advanced than we think. At this point, establishing knowledge benchmarks that retards the immature brain, or expecting regurgitation of information with a potential negative experience that sorts children into an inescapable intellectual prison is not productive.

Children have the right to their own intellectual destiny. By presuming to know what every child needs to learn to succeed, we take that right away. Knowledge should be offered up on a plate of curiosity and allowed to be sampled.

Knowledge attained for the purpose of a grade dissipates. Knowledge attained out of curiosity fuels inspiration.

It seems quite premature to test, grade, sort, and stigmatize an immature brain. The immature brain seems to be like an unformatted computer disk. By experiencing the world around them, children are formatting their disk to accept knowledge. Trying to put the knowledge in before the disk is formatted is like putting the cart before the horse.

What is the environment like where the immature brain thrives? Play is the historical way children learn the adult behaviors that are required to survive. Play is still one of the most powerful activities to support learning. Sadly, play is only associated with a break from learning. This is such a lost opportunity. The classroom and playground should be full of play and learning opportunities. In fact, I could see some children spending the majority of their school day in a playground-learning environment.

A child discovery center would best define an immature brain-learning environment. Nowhere should there be the stifling effects of the arrogant and insecure behavior of sorting, testing and categorizing. In order to support the immature brain we must have Faith in the natural learning process and provide the rich environment of fascination, curiosity and individuality

The Mature Brain

Structured and goal-oriented learning is exactly what the mature brain needs. It has become aware of the world. It has become aware of the need to sustain itself and draws from the unique tendencies developed during the immature brain development. In essence, the mature brain knows what it likes to do and becomes more willing to do what it might have not wanted to do in order to succeed.

Standard teaching practices actually appeal to the mature brain. The mature brain has developed a sense of purpose. The mature brain has become goal-oriented. The mature brain still negatively responds to being overwhelmed, but still likes to be challenged and stimulated by curiosity. The mature brain can will itself to understand something if it is relevant to a priority interest. The mature brains potential to learn is tied to the type of environment the immature brain developed in.

Some critical aspects of brain maturity are that there are two totally different learning approaches to the two brain conditions. The maturity rate is different in all children and the maturity rate varies by subject in each child.

There is no way for a grade level system to respond to this reality. The best system provided by the public school system was the one room school house. A child would progress without the pressures of grade level. Each subject progressed independent of a child's age.

The speed at which a mature brain absorbs information is of no importance, what is important is the mature brains enthusiasm for a subject. That enthusiasm is an indication that the child's brain has a purpose for that information regardless of how fast it is being absorbed.

Primary and Secondary Interest and Information

An immature brain spends a lot of time searching for primary interests. Primary interests are mysterious information journeys children are compelled to follow, powered by internal motivation.

When we direct a child's attention away from this process we take away the child's right to their own intellectual destiny. In doing so, we take the child's internal motivation away and have to replace it with external motivation.

Imagine a child's learning process like a path and primary interests is a child's flashlight that allows the child the ability to see the path. When we take the flashlight away they cannot see the path and have to rely on someone to guide them - only it is no longer the path they should be on.

Secondary interests and information supports primary interests and is typically a skill or information that supports a primary interest. Our current school system is trying to put in secondary information into our children's immature brains before the child has developed their primary interests. Secondary information does not absorb very well if primary information is not already well embedded in a child's brain.

To some degree we can identify primary and secondary information. Children find the natural world to be a primary interest and a math or a communication skill to be a secondary interest. This is not always the case, though. Our school system actually supports very well children whose primary interests are math or communication skills. It is important to note that, after a brain matures and it has developed primary interests, secondary information is easy to absorb.

Internal Motivation

A child can study for a test and pass only to retain half of what was learned to pass. The motivation to learn was to pass the test. Some children's motivation to learn is to please adults. Motivation and where it comes from is the most important element in success.

Individuals up against insurmountable odds succeed because of internal motivation. Knowledge gained by internal motivation is rarely lost. Internal motivation accelerates the learning process. Internal motivation puts purpose in knowledge. External motivation can get you through a test, it can get you through the day at work, it can help you win a game, but it will not help you succeed in life. It is a mystery where internal motivation comes from. Can we help children find internal motivation? I think we can, but the current school system suppresses it. The fundamental right of a child to their own intellectual path is at the heart of internal motivation. You can lead a horse to water but you can't make it drink. This reality is at the heart of internal motivation. Leading someone around creates apathy; creating an atmosphere of wonderment triggers a desire to explore; the desire to explore stimulates internal motivation. It's like perpetual motion; once you get it started it generates its own energy.

Think about all the important events of civilization. Internal motivation was at the heart of these events. What becomes of a society if people don't have internal motivation? I think if internal motivation is suppressed for too long by oppressive activities people rebel in an effort to remove the oppression. This is not a very productive learning environment.

Positive Reinforcement

A lot of people support the A, B, C, D and F system of grading. They would argue that children need to know where they are doing well and where they are doing poorly. They would argue that children need an incentive to do well.

Adopting this misguided system is proof that the system is only able to look at learning from one point of view and it is not the child's. The child that gets the A or B gets positive reinforcement and the child that gets the C, D, and F gets negative reinforcement. The argument then implies that the student is lazy, not applying himself or in need of special intervention. This is a self-fulfilling prophesy for a lot of children. The system creates the reality it finds itself in. All levels of progression need to have positive reinforcement. It's a right that needs to be extended to all children. Not extending it proves how inadequate our current system is.

In order to understand how important this principle is to learning, imagine a long flight of stairs. At each step it is important to encourage a child to make the next step. If a child is punished with a blow to his or her self-esteem, their desire to take the next step decreases. Every time this happens there is erosion of their desire to learn. This erosion can follow the child into adulthood. Failure should not be an occasion to punish; rather, it should be an occasion for positive reinforcement. To err is to learn. Encouraging a child when they have failed teaches them that principle.

Fear of failing can become one of the biggest handicaps adults can carry with them through life. We should not be afraid of failing. We should embrace it as a form of knowledge.

A less oppressive system would be made up of levels - perhaps 1 through 5. In each learning discipline, a child could be evaluated by a level. As one progresses one gets closer to the optimum level, eliminating the negative form in assessments. Just like a set of stairs, each success or failure gets you closer to the top.

Do not create an environment riddled with opportunities to punish failure. Do not create an environment with winners and losers. The winning and losing environment has no place in a learning environment.

Daydreaming

This was my favorite pastime in school. Unfortunately it was frowned upon. This is understandable. Someone was trying to share his or her knowledge with me, and I was not paying attention. I felt I was doing something very important.

How many of you daydream? I like to think daydreaming is the brain making intellectual soup. The brain takes information from different mediums and puts that information together. Sometimes the soup is good and sometimes the soup is useless. This process needs to be legitimized by any future school system. Daydreaming will give us creative solutions to our future problems. Daydreaming will give our children a form of happiness and confidence associated with unlimited possibilities.

The current school system is in direct conflict with daydreaming. A student constantly has to be aware of what a teacher is doing in order to take advantage of the teaching technique. Guess what? Children do not have that kind of attention span, so why do we force them?

The current school system expects unnatural behavior from children. Since children are hardwired to learn, why is it necessary to impose a system that does not work in harmony with their natural processes? You will see this form of incompatibility throughout our current school system. A natural learning environment is like pushing a round stone, and the current learning environment is like pushing a flat stone. Which would you rather be pushing? If learning was the only goal, this analogy would be enough. The reality is that the human learning experience is so multifaceted that characterizing it as pushing a stone is an injustice.

Daydreaming is but another example of the complexity of the natural learning ability of children that we do not enable because it is not useful in our current school system.

Trial and Error

This form of learning is completely underestimated. Our school system even goes so far as to punish this form of learning. Maybe it is considered to be a primitive form of learning.

Watch children. Trial and error is their favorite form of learning. It's full of curiosity and fascination. One of its downfalls, and probably why our current school system tends not to use it, is it's difficult to test knowledge gained by trial and error.

The knowledge gained by trial and error creates a solid foundation for success and happiness. Trial and error is a fundamental technique for scientists to gain an understanding of our world. Within a trial and error environment a child is not punished by failure but taught by failure.

Our current school system teaches us to be afraid of failure, but failure is merely a reinforcement of the eventual correct knowledge and a form of disk formatting. Our brains use experiences to tie knowledge to memory. Failure is just another experience we can use.

We no longer can use failure if we punish it. Even in a natural environment we can become afraid of something because of the negative effects of trial and error. In fact we should. When we touch something hot, it hurts and we do not touch it again. When a child gets punished for failing in school what is their response? They become afraid if it.

Watch children playing a video game. Notice how motivated they are to play video games. It would be incredible if we could capture that enthusiasm in the classroom. Children can play for hours learning a game without any external motivation.

I believe the games are appealing to a child's desire for trial and error learning.

By understanding the power of trial and error we can unleash a force for learning that will encourage our children to new heights. We must incorporate this form of learning into the future school system. It is going to take some trial and error to develop a system, but the benefits will be worth it.

Physical Activity and Learning

For children, these two processes go hand-in-hand. Children are learning about physics when they run, play, jump and roll around. Children touch, smell and taste everything. They have a strong desire to immerse themselves physically in the learning process. Who in the world thought it would be a good idea to sit a child down to teach them something? I think we are missing a huge opportunity to expand our children's minds on the playground and in the school room.

Why not design school playground equipment to teach? If we did we would be creating a powerful learning environment. Imagine children in play mode developing basic understanding for complicated concepts for physics, math and science.

Let's remove the desks and design learning concepts around touching, seeing, smelling and tasting. I know this sounds weird, but the more senses that are stimulated in a learning environment, the easier the information is remembered because there are multiple pathways created in the brain to the stored location of the information. I believe our brains absorb everything, but we cannot retrieve all the information because we have not created pathways back to the location to retrieve it. This could be why children seem to retain so well when physical and other stimulating activities are combined in a learning environment.

Learning by Observing

I have always worried what my children were learning by watching me. I have not always exhibited the traits I would like my children to exhibit. Children also learn by observing other children. Both of these scenarios scare me. We know children learn by observation, but we do not take full advantage of this form of learning.

Even though children learn by observing naturally, there is an opportunity to evolve the natural learning process of observation by legitimizing its power and encouraging a child to evolve their own learning process.

Watch and learn. I love that phrase. So much of what a child has to learn about life can be learned by observing. In order for observations to be of value a child needs to develop a technique for processing the information. Because we have not legitimized learning by observation too many children do not have the processing apparatus to assess the observations. Peer pressure, undeveloped standards and weak personal identity can make a child vulnerable to life situations that have powerful observational influences.

I believe that if we legitimize this learning process and show our children how to evaluate this type of knowledge, then we can give our children a fun way to learn and a learning tool for life.

Be Happy

Parents want their children to be happy. Learning makes children happy. If we want to measure how well our children are learning, we should measure their happiness, or measure their enthusiasm for school each day.

What would it be like if our children got up each day excited to go to school? Children learn best when they are happy. How much happiness is in our school system? Are our teachers happy? The happiness that comes from learning fuels the desire to learn more; it becomes infectious. Other children, and most important, teachers, are energized by this happiness. If a child is not happy to go to school and a parent is the one making him or her go, what does this do to that relationship?

There is no test required to measure happiness. A measuring system could be done daily very easily without expense. In fact, parents already do this measuring instinctively. Their child's lack of happiness is the first red flag that goes up which starts parents thinking about home schooling. How do you create a happy learning environment? You do it by enabling the natural learning process.

Social Skills

This is the most common concern among parents thinking of home-schooling. Parents worry their children will not develop their social skills without going to school. What are social skills? Social skills are a child's ability to communicate and fit in. I am not sure what social skills children have to offer other children except maybe bad social skills.

I think adults need to develop better social skills like empathy, compassion, communication, dependability, listening and then be the examples for our children's social skills.

Why do we not see the potential for children to help other children learn what we have taught them, while we think it is ok for children that have not developed social skills to teach other children social skills? I believe good social skills develop naturally in a learning environment of cooperation. Older children helping younger children and children working together on learning projects support good social skills. If success depends on our ability to get along it stands to reason that we will develop good social skills to get along. If success depends on beating the other child then children will develop poor social skills designed to overpower other children.

The Kid Culture

When our teaching presentation is unappealing, children start exhibiting apathy. This also happens when a child begins to slip behind in a goal-oriented school system. Apathy is the driving force behind the kid culture. The kid culture is like a safety net for a child's emotions. The kid culture is the barrier that protects their self-esteem. The kid culture is the motivation they create to go to school everyday. The kid culture is the chaos they create to entertain their brain. The kid culture can manifest itself in many forms.

The problem with the kid culture is it interferes with the ability to engage with our children. The process of developing the kid culture begins in grade school, and by the time children get to high school it becomes a formidable barrier to the learning process. School systems even have to accommodate for it by activities designed to pacify the culture.

Disrespect, a lack of gratitude and motivation is the poison the kid culture brings to school. Most of the negative manifestation of the kid culture should dissipate in a natural learning environment, replaced by a child's internal motivation and enthusiasm for knowledge. The positive effects would be enormous. High school would resemble a college campus. Teenagers would be charting their intellectual journey attending classes with purpose. Children would appreciate the efforts of their community for providing them an education. Going to school would be uplifting for both children and teachers. Children would be fascinated with the real world again.

The Value of a Community

The more open and inviting a school system is, the more the community will get involved. The community is where a child should develop their social skills, not from the kid culture. The community has the diversity of age. The community has the connection to the real world. The community has abundant resources for children to experience real life activities.

Involving the community does not mean going to the Christmas play or going to the sporting events. Involving the community in the mentoring of children means making the two world's one.

Have you ever had a person come up to you and blow you away when they tell you how kind or motivated or respectful your child is, when around you they do not exhibit these behaviors?

I think children begin at an early age to develop socially accepted behavior around other people, like a self-molding process for the purpose of being accepted. That is why it is important for children to be around other adult worlds other than the one at home or the one at school.

In our modern society we have created invisible barriers -- barriers between children and adults, barriers between children and the real world, barriers between children and the elderly, barriers between children and work, barriers between our children and governing bodies and barriers between children and learning.

The school system should be the heart of the community, a heart that sends its life-supporting nutrients throughout the community. I think this process would tear down all the barriers we currently experience.

For Your Information

Mankind has amassed an enormous amount of information. What do we do with this information? Information alone is useless. There is something very important that needs to be added to information to make it valuable (wisdom). When you add wisdom to information, the information becomes knowledge. A child's early years should be spent in self-discovery; self-discovery leads to wisdom. Self-discovery is accomplished by experiencing life. Combining wisdom with information creates knowledge. When you have knowledge instead of information, you can mold life into a rich and fulfilling experience. Without knowledge, life can become a sterile and depressing place.

Most children do not absorb information well without having a reasonable amount of time in self-discovery. Children that can absorb information without time spent in self-discovery lack the ability to use it wisely.

Interacting with life will give us a perspective that is critical for us to charter a course in life. By discovering life we can respond to it. This process reveals and molds our personality. Children have to decide what type of information they will gather and what they will do with that information. If they do not have the ability to do that, the information becomes useless and charting a course becomes difficult.

Oppression and Discrimination

Oppression and discrimination have followed mankind since the beginning of time. Its origin comes from a variety of human dysfunctions. Our founding fathers put a Bill of Rights into founding documents to stem the tide of oppression and discrimination. The Bill of Rights has had a significant impact on curbing oppression and discrimination in our country. By greatly reducing the effects of oppression and discrimination, we have come closer to realizing mankind's full potential.

Although our society has discovered the benefits of removing oppression and discrimination from our adult lives, we have not noticed its existence in our school system. We tend to have an over simplified view of our children's role in life and limited sense of responsibility towards them. It is time to extend the same respect and rights we give ourselves to our children.

The freedom of our children to choose their own intellectual destiny, to follow their individual path, to not be sorted, classified and stigmatized and to absorb information without parameters are just a few rights that should be extended to our children.

Freedom has given our country so many blessings. What would freedom do for our children? The only way to find out is to extend that freedom to our children. There is no way to predict the path freedom would lead our children down, but our founding fathers did not know where freedom would lead us- but knew it was the right thing to do.

Learning Is a Process, Not a System

A process has its own timetable, and in each child there is a different timetable. If you remove a step in the process, the process slows down dramatically. To prevent disabling the natural learning process it is important to understand it. Understanding the natural learning process is critical in order to enable it to proceed.

One important observation about the natural learning process is that an immature brain is different than the mature brain. The fundamental process for an immature brain is like formatting a computer disk to receive information; where as the process for a mature brain requires the mature brain to have a formatted disk ready to receive information. Children know how to format their disks naturally; they use their curiosity about the world around them. If the disk is receiving information, the child is happy. If the disk does not, the child can become depressed. Formatting a child's disk is the process of exposing them to all of the fascinating facets of life. No testing, no evaluating needed. A child does it naturally. There will be time enough when a brain matures to help evaluate the strategic importance of knowledge. There will be time enough to chart a course for success. Confidence in the process will give everyone piece of mind.

Children are preprogrammed with this natural learning process, which is tied to their overall health. If we do not enable the natural learning process, children become sick- maybe not so sick that we would notice right away, but over time, which makes it hard to detect.

Why would we not want to design a school system that would support the natural learning process? Maybe we don't understand the natural learning process. Maybe our need to track progress is more important. Maybe we are so arrogant that we think that we can create a better process than the natural one.

Little Things are Big Things

Life is in the details. Little things combine together to fill our lives with true joy and happiness. Like a symphony, every instrument combines to create something beautiful. Like a painting every brush stroke combines to reveal a masterpiece. It is the same in learning. If you sterilize the learning environment by limiting the learning options, it will become impossible to recognize true knowledge and what its purpose is for each child. We need to legitimize all children and their optimal learning approach.

Making all children conform to a primitive educational system sterilizes our lives. It forces some children to reject society. It forces some children to subdue their real potential. The little details of learning need to be more important than the system we employ to teach. The current school system is so big and complicated that it takes center stage. A future system needs to be simple. For it to be simple it will have to embrace the simple wisdom of faith. Little things are simple; combine all the little things and you will find yourself at the end of your quest.

When I was a young boy, my brother and I would go out into the woods in the spring when there were still snow piles on the dirt roads. Our goal was to try very hard not to get stuck. Eventually, after a lot of fun and exciting snowdrift-busting we would get stuck. Not one idea would relieve the '50 Chevy from its icy prison. I would have an idea; my brother would have an idea. We would discuss the ideas and which one would be the best. Usually two or three more ideas would surface. After awhile the decision to use all of the ideas at the same time would extricate the truck from its precarious position. I bring up this boyhood memory to illustrate the power of using multiple assets at one time. To achieve our education goals, we have to be willing to look at multiple learning assets or techniques. To employ only one is to abandon the '50 Chevy and walk home.

The "You Got To" Syndrome

How do children respond to being told they have to do something? When they are young they try to accommodate, but sooner or later they begin to rebel. The need to make their own decisions becomes so important that they are willing to choose the opposite of what they are told to do.

The freedom to choose is at the core of a child's personal identity. When a child is young they have no life experiences to make an informed decision. Parents take over this responsibility for awhile. Parents can tell you that, not too long into the rearing process, they had to replace "you got to" with some form of negotiation. The "You Got To" syndrome unfortunately follows our children through grade school and high school.

I wonder if this form of motivation creates in people a form of apathy, only acting when life makes them do something. I wonder if our need to escape our "got to" world is why we embrace our vacations, movies, TV and games. Is this natural or have we - by the way we force our goals on children - created this behavior? Could a different environment produce a person that embraced their life and finding enjoyment simply living their life? Life is quite interesting; we should not make it a got-to-do activity. We should learn to draw a child's attention to life and all its wonderment by not sterilizing it.

Passive Entertainment and the Unreal World

The competition for our children's attention is getting tough. I am afraid if we do not find a way to recapture our children's fascination with life they will permanently embrace the unreal world throughout their adult life.

What kind of a human being will this be? Technology continues to improve its ability to entertain. It is hard to imagine that technology can even compete with life.

I believe the way we educate our children has a lot to do with the unreal world's success in capturing our children's attention. The desire for passive entertainment thrives in an environment where individuals find what they do each day to be undesirable -- a routine that becomes depressing. Whatever comes along that provides an escape becomes an instant success.

The only way to get through this life is to engage it. Why not teach our children to find fascination around every corner? You can only ignore the real world for so long before it starts having a negative impact on your life. Engage with life and it will have a positive impact on you. If someone could just invent a video game that made the player feel emotion, pain, see three dimensional images they could make a mint – oh, we already have that game: life.

Qualities of a Person

Where do qualities of a person come from? Does our current school system nurture them? What are they? Are they important? I think our current school system would like attentiveness in children as a quality.

Qualities are actually quite important. The qualities of a person set the tone for a successful learning environment. Some of these qualities are gratitude, respect, humility, kindness, empathy, happiness, optimism, persistence, compassion, etc.

The fact is our current school system does not teach or nurture most of the important qualities a child needs to succeed in life. I think most of the important human qualities will mature in a natural learning environment because they are already in the child. I think the way in which we approach children with knowledge plays a huge role in children developing their natural human qualities.

The free flow of the natural learning environment provides an excellent opportunity to inject other human qualities that might not evolve on their own. Children need to know that a school system legitimizes these qualities. A school system needs to have a strategic plan for creating an environment that nurtures good human qualities.

A Formula for Success

We will never know what each individual will need to know to succeed in life. The simple skills we struggle to implant in our children will help, but they alone will not accomplish this goal. By ignoring the individual potential and focusing on these skills we have given the impression that they alone will create success. These skills we try to implant in an immature brain for a mature brain are not even a challenge if you have not already preconditioned a child to think they are hard.

Developing a child's formula for success, starts very early in a child's life. Each child will assemble a different formula. It starts during the immature brain development. It has nothing to do originally with learned skills. If during this time a child is overwhelmed with outside forces trying to define success for them the natural process of developing a formula will stop.

Faith is very important during immature brain development and confidence in the complex power of each child's brain is essential. An immature brain is in constant learning mode if we do not mess with it.

Monetary gain cannot be the defining parameters for success. The concept of making money does not stimulate a child's brain to learn. The confusion comes from the adult world that is struggling to make money or that recognizes that a lot of money provides power. Before you take a trip you better make sure you have a vehicle to get there and make sure the vehicle is the one you want to go in. Making money for money's sake can make a person sick. Making money residually doing something you love can uplift the soul. As a society we put way to much importance on monetary gain. Instead our emphasis should be on helping our children sustain themselves on very little. That skill will be a great asset while they discover a formula for success.

Analogies

Analogies are a great way to help us get our minds around an elusive concept. We use them all the time in our everyday lives. Even though they are very useful, they can also lead us astray. Sometimes 80 percent of an analogy fits the subject, but 20 percent may not. That 20 percent can skew the analogies just enough so we still buy into it, but it leads us away from success. The following are some analogies I think you will find interesting. The analogy can sound logical but be totally out of touch with reality or they can be right on:

School is like a race; you don't want to fall behind

Imagine your child is behind. As a parent, if school is like a race and your child is falling behind the others, you feel the need to encourage your child to catch up. You don't want your child to lose or not finish. We have been conditioned to fear this scenario.

Life is a journey; everyone has a different path.

This analogy is in direct conflict with the first. In this analogy, our paths are different, and not like a race at all. It is impossible to get behind because no one is in front and impossible to win because no one is behind you. Imagine the power of personal inspiration guiding them down their paths.

A child is like a seed.

Give a child what they need to grow and they will grow all on their own. We don't have to monitor a child if we give them a learning environment that they thrive in.

A child is like a sponge, absorbing everything in sight.

In this analogy, the child is empowered to learn by their own capabilities.

A child's brain is like an empty drum that needs to be filled.

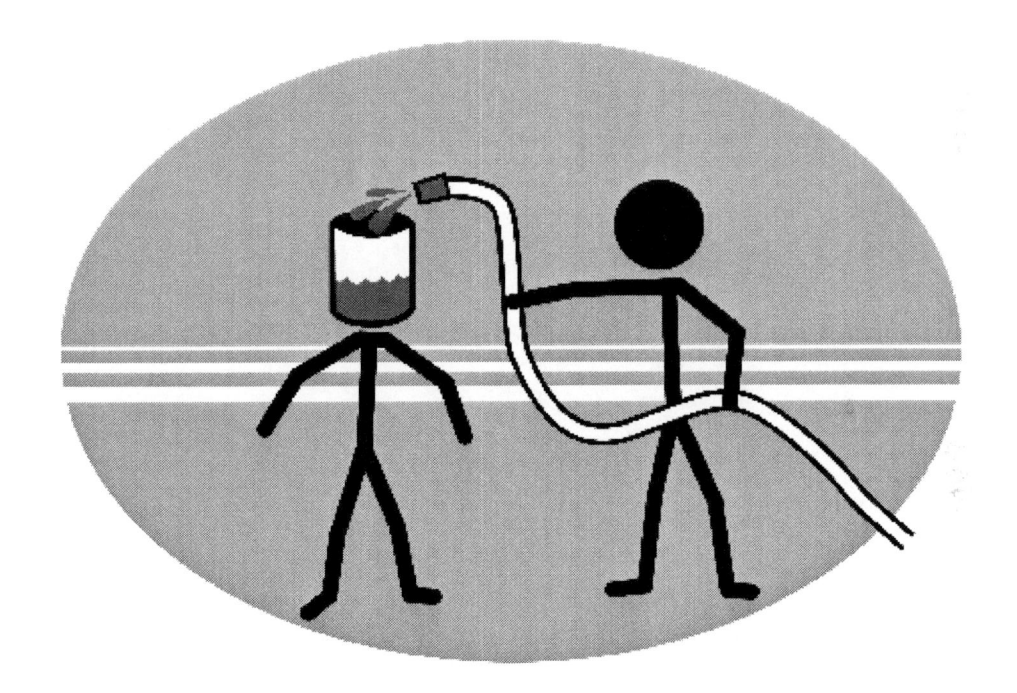

In this analogy, we need to put things into our children's brains, or there will not be anything in there.

Life is a hard road and we need to prepare our children for it.

In this analogy, if we don't give our children what they need, they might fail.

Life is like an obstacle course full of challenges that create a purposeful life.

In this analogy, life is a gift.

Life is like a ladder; you have to crawl over somebody to move up.

In this analogy, there are winners and losers and who cares about the losers.

Life is like a long flight of stairs; there is plenty of room to gather on each stair to share your experiences with people on the way up.

In this analogy, people are helping and learning from each other.

Life is like a game; in order to succeed in life you need to win.

In this analogy, someone needs to lose in order for you to win.

Life is a destination; you need to hurry up and get there.

In this analogy, how do you know you have reached your destination?

Life is a journey; you need to enjoy every step of the way.

The natural learning environment lives in this analogy.

I Can Only Imagine

Let's try to imagine what a natural learning school system might look like. Creating the natural world in a building is obviously impossible but the order of the stimulation and the elements that create curiosity in the real world can be recreated in a building. In fact we can even speed up the exposure and be more selective than the natural world. As long as the experiences have a real attachment to the natural world and not synthesized to being tasks a child might need, an indoor learning experience can be very similar to the natural world. As children mature they can actually engage with the natural world as part of their learning environment.

Remember we have buildings, personnel and capital. I would keep the grouping of ages, elementary school, middle school and high school. Each of the three categories has their own strategic purpose. Elementary school is the immature brain development period. The middle school is the transition period when the immature brain is developing into a mature brain. And high school is where the mature brain begins its life-long quest for knowledge.

Elementary School

Because children develop at different rates, grade school should function more like a one room schoolhouse with children of varying ages mingling through the day. Children should be allowed to move throughout the school, or, more appropriately, child discovery center. Science rooms, math rooms, music rooms, art rooms, history rooms, english rooms, invention room, hobby rooms, construction rooms, green house, playground, library and lunchroom are all designed around a hands on; interactive exposure to life. In this learning environment, the building becomes a learning resource.

As older children begin to engage with teachers, younger children listen and begin to learn even faster than their predecessors. Older children, anxious to show off their newfound knowledge, begin to instruct younger children. Teachers should be able to engage children in small groups or one on one. Teachers are allowed time to develop techniques to attract children's curiosity in their specialty, but teachers can mingle throughout the discovery center because a child might respond better to one personality over another.

There could be a level system like a set of stairs that, for each subject, evaluates a child's traceable knowledge. There can be a testing room where children can, by their own choice, take tests for fun and learning or tests to evaluate the level they have achieved in a traditional or nontraditional subject. Evaluations can be valuable for teachers to identify where they need to adjust their content. But remember, evaluations can be misleading and have no relevance in evaluating a child's intelligence. Children need to continuously engage the big picture without the constraints of a small picture evaluation. If we become too preoccupied with details, some children will appear to be behind when they are not and their learning processes will slow way down.

In almost anything a child gets interested in there is an opportunity to teach all subjects. This fundamental reality will enable a teacher to expand upon a child's interest to encompass a well-rounded education, even if a child only shows interest in one area of a child discovery center.

Because there is a loose structure or free flow to this format, children can focus in on interests and parents can easily interface with children as easily as a teacher. The discovery center could be available six days a week, maybe open from 8 a.m. to 8 p.m. to allow parents an opportunity to participate in their child's learning at the discovery center. Home-schoolers could use the resources of the discovery center as well and consider the school system merely as another resource for learning.

Middle School

Middle school is where there would be a focused effort to evaluate a child and expose them to a more formal classroom setting. A child of any age, in any subject, can participate in middle school if they are ready. He or she would learn skills specifically for articulating around a mature brain-learning environment.

This is a transition time, a time for a child to think about and learn how they will participate and engage in life. This is a time to legitimize any life pursuit, even if it does not involve monetary gain. This is a time when a child, if they have not already done so, might start thinking about their interface with life. During this time, a child might spend more time in the community to help organize and focus their knowledge towards a specific direction.

High School

High school, or more appropriately named, our community adult learning center, would be similar to college; children would choose their classes either for college prep or for an individual, unique purpose. Like grade school there would be no mandatory testing. Testing would be voluntary for the purpose of evaluating proficiency. There could be proficiency levels for general life, for college, for business, for farming, etc. If a child chose not to ever be tested and wanted to just continue taking classes for the pure joy of it, they could.

If adults wanted to take classes, they could -- almost like a community college. Keeping the mandatory testing out of the community adult learning center allows the momentum created during grade school to continue. Test only when a person wants to establish a proficiency level. This approach would make testing incredibly more efficient and would remove any stigmatism testing generally creates.

A child would not have to go to school all day. They could choose a work study program, learning expeditions, a community service program or an outdoor recreation program. The idea of being in school is always available to the child as they discover the value of an education. Allowing for a well-rounded exposure to life provides an opportunity for an individual to express his or her own intellectual destiny. Throughout a learning environment, for all ages, it is important to create an environment that stimulates curiosity, even if a student has not found a path in life. Throughout grade school and high school there should be resources that keep children fascinated with learning. The community learning center should attract all ages of the community to classes by providing an opportunity for them to learn and share their knowledge with others, thereby communicating to all children that the process of learning is a lifelong journey.

Research and Development

Any large corporation with a future will have a "research and development" division. The purpose is to refine what they do, to find new and better ways of doing what they do. All of the concepts I have proposed are untested. Even though they ring true, the benefits of them in a group environment, interfacing with adults and an infrastructure, will take trial and error and a belief that we can improve our children's learning environment.

We must invest time in understanding these observations and develop a system to take advantage of their benefits.

It is easy to become frustrated with something new. It is important to give it time to succeed. If we approach the current school system like it has approached our children's education the current school system will become frustrated, apathetic and resistant to learn. It will take time, patience and understanding. The current system will not come around instantly. It is important to start experimenting with these observations to begin improving our public school system. Confidence in a new system will come from one success at a time.

The Jelling and Healing Affects of a Family Learning Together

We should provide the opportunity for families to be involved together in a learning environment. We should create an opportunity to do things with our families that we have never been able to do before in school. A frustrating homework session between parents and children is not what I am referring to.

Being a family in today's world is a challenge. Families are naturally vulnerable to a host of dysfunctional manifestations. Add the pressures of our daily life and there is potential for disaster. Providing a venue for family bonding would help greatly.

A system should not require parent's involvement but remove barriers and provide opportunities for families to engage in learning activities. The current school system even sees parental involvement as an asset for teaching children. I think this is only the tip of the iceberg as far as what could be accomplished by providing an environment for families to learn together.

After my wife and I took our kids out of school I became addicted to moments when my children would comprehend something I was trying to explain to them. A special bond developed that I had never felt with them before.

Life before home-schooling was a routine of forcefully engaging with our children to "eat", "get to school" and "get your homework done" relationship. I cannot imagine what my relationship would have been with my children if we had not home-schooled them.

If only our children were excited to go to school and parents felt motivated to experience that magical connection of being involved with their children's knowledge. What a great source for happiness that we don't currently have on a large scale.

Children Are Our Future

"Children are our future." No truer statement has ever been made. Sadly, the statement is made to justify spending more money on the current system but to no effect.

What do we want our children's future to be? Parents want it to be a future of their child's making. Parents want their children to have tools to build that future. Parents want their children to have confidence, moral judgment, compassion, creativity and dedication. Parents do not want their children to be limited in their options.

The school system we currently have has encouraged the creation of a macro world: huge corporations and huge governments. I would like to see our children build a future that is not so sterile -- one that is small enough to bring back the richness of the human experience. I would like our children to be invulnerable to the mistakes of a few people -- a world small enough to empower the individual to make a positive impact on the world around them.

Should we be the engineers of our children's future or should our children be the engineers of their own future? Do we know what is best for our children or do they? Have we succeeded so well that we want our children to follow our example? Maybe we should say the future is our children's.

I want our children to improve on what we have done. I want them to have confidence. I want them to be creative. I want them to be happy.

The future looks to be more challenging than any other time in history. Every child will count. In the future the idea that we can sort out the smartest children, and they will carry the human race forward, is a lose-lose scenario. The idea that children show their true potential in early years must be abandoned. The choices and the honesty we exhibit now will have a profound impact on the future. The children are our future.

In the Future

The cost to educate a child does not have to be so high. The natural learning process could cut education expenses drastically, leaving surplus capital for teachers or learning aids.

A more efficient school system would be less of a burden on society. In the future there might not be the capital we have now. School systems could adapt easily to less money and still provide a high quality education.

I see, in the future, parents' going to their child's discovery center to observe and participate in their child's learning experience. I see a community providing experiences that help children format their disks. I see a separate and highly specialized system becoming integrated back into a community. I see the federal government out of schools. I see children with an enthusiasm and passion for life. I see children going to a retirement home to learn from senior citizens. I see children connected to the fabric of life. I see children who respect others. I see children climbing mountains, kayaking rivers, scuba diving, and sailing. I see high schools becoming adult education centers and providing classes to the community. I see student-exchange programs around the country providing a diverse opportunity for all students to learn from other communities. I see playgrounds that teach. I see schools that provide a learning environment all year long. I see teachers loving their jobs again. I see children learning fiscal responsibilities. I see children learning important life skills. I see older children helping younger children to learn. I see classrooms coming alive with history, science, math, english, engineering, problem solving, building and creativity. I see night classes with telescopes pointing into the night sky. I see children working part time to save up for college or an investment account. I want to see all the ideas other people come up with to facilitate the natural learning process incorporated into our schools.

The Future Vacation

Fun is not the first thing you think of when you think of learning, but there is a vacation-like effect when we learn for the simple pleasure of learning. When there is no grade and no monetary gain and when there is no ulterior motivation other than the opportunity to expand our minds, learning takes on a whole new dynamic. In fact, the feeling we can get from learning this way is quite uplifting.

Learning for the fun of learning is not new. Families have been taking vacations to Yellowstone National Park and other national parks to learn about our natural surroundings for generations. People take eco trips for the same purpose. To a great degree, through our school system, we have programmed people not to think of learning as an enjoyable activity. In the future, after we have embraced the natural learning process, businesses might see the opportunity to profit from learning vacations. Colleges might spring up that provide lectures, labs and learning environments for the pure purpose of learning, not for grades nor for a degree, and no negative or purposeful constraints -- just learning for the pure joy of learning.

What is the Human Experience?

Who am I? Why am I here? These are hard questions to answer. I would start by observing nature. It appears that all living things learn by adaptation. Adaptation is a form of intelligence. That would suggest that all living things have a form of intelligence. Learning appears to be a common thread in all living forms. Learning, then, can be the basis for understanding the question, "Why am I here?"

The human experience is the most dynamic of all living things. We can see similarities to other large mammals, but recognize a large gap between their experience and ours. Our experience seems to be a journey of self-discovery. Is this the answer to the question, "Why am I here?" I am here to discover myself, is that it?

Who am I? If I am here to discover myself, then that question will be answered. While I am here, I will discover who I am. This perspective puts the importance of school into a whole new category. Those in charge of the school system have to understand the larger picture of the human experience and the role learning plays in that picture. The role of school can help in the path to self-discovery, or it can seriously handicap it. I believe we all have a unique path to self discovery. I believe we are hard-wired with a path map that helps us down that path. No organization or person will ever know another person's path. That is the basis for the statement, "Every child has the right to their own intellectual destiny." Without that right, we have taken away from our children the purpose of life.

A Change Will Do You Good

Why do some people accept things the way they are and other people look for and are excited about finding better ways to do things? In times when we have to accept things the way they are, it is important to have the state of mind to endure them; this is a helpful human trait. While we are enduring, there is nothing wrong with pursuing inspiration for ways to improve things. I think all children are born with both of these human traits. I think disappointment, the need to conform or the fear of failing could be why a lot of us hold on to the human trait of enduring and abandon the human trait of what could be. Some people can endure and have the desire to pursue better ways of doing things, while other people have embraced their ability to endure and have abandoned trying to make things better.

A child's brain is a learning miracle. A child's brain has hard wired processes that we will never understand, and are so complex that when we put a child into a rigid curriculum the child has to disable most of them to conform. My definition of a curriculum: an organized attempt to assimilate the natural world into our children in an unnatural way. Some children resist this disabling process. Some of these children are considered to be learning disabled, some are considered to be disruptive, some lazy and some bullies. Most children just disable them and conform. Children that turn them off are embraced by our school system and therefore given positive reinforcement by embracing the human trait of acceptance and a life long abandonment of what could have been.

Some children resisted the brain-disabling effects they experienced in school. Even though they did poorly in school, the school experience did not dictate how they did in life; in fact, holding onto the human trait of what could be, catapulted them into a great deal of success.

We should never disable natural brain processes, instead we should provide for their development. So many of the brain processes are unique to the child, a curriculum can never support them. We need an environment that provides resources for their development. Those resources are found all around us in the environment that the brain evolved in. It is a very complex, sensory rich and diverse environment. A natural environment possesses all of the checks and balances that curriculums so poorly try to emulate. A natural learning environment stimulates internal motivation. A natural learning environment allows for selective learning so important to a child's self discovery. A natural learning environment does not disable brain processes. A natural learning environment molds and develops them.

Options

Have you ever been faced with a problem that seemed impossible to solve? Then, after you thought about it for a while, you came up with a possible solution? After you thought about it for a while longer, you came up with more options. Our brains are very resourceful. The brains of children are very resourceful too. A child might find a way to learn something in an unorthodox way. He or she may not conform to our way of thinking, but an option a child creates to learn may work very well. Children problem-solve constantly. If we don't let children exercise this part of their brain, they will never develop it.

Letting children come up with their own options to solve a learning challenge customizes the knowledge to the way the child's brain processes information. If we de-legitimize a child's option-creating processes, we will take away the child's confidence. I am not sure why, but without confidence there are disabling effects to our ability to use our knowledge. Pre-empting a child when they are problem solving with prior knowledge or a different or better way tend to stifle a child's option creation process and take their confidence away. An athlete is a good example of the need for confidence in our ability. If confidence is lost, their performance is severely disabled.

The Truth is Hidden or We Would Not Be Able to Find It

The simple wisdom in this statement is so profoundly infused in understanding our journey through life that I use it everyday. I am always humbled by the fact that truth is simple. We tend to make life more complicated than we need to make it. We can actually hide the truth ourselves by making life too complicated. Why is truth so important? Why do we give up on it? Do all people look for it? What will finding truth do for us? I look at truth like a puzzle; each piece represents a truth I have found. As I find a place to connect that piece with the other pieces I have found, I become a little more humble. As I gather pieces and look at the picture the puzzle is making, I see that I have been helped all along the way to find these pieces of truth. The forces that hide the truths from me helped me to understand the truths when I find them. One of the truths I have found is that children learn naturally. I have come to this understanding, because our school system hid it behind a complex and uninspired system. In other words, we must feel the cold so we can pursue the warmth. Sometimes you have to fail in order to understand how to succeed. The feeling that failure gives is the need to find the truth. The desire for truth prompts us to abandon a little more of ourselves and embrace faith as a compass instead of worldly pursuits. Hidden in the fabric of life found only by faith, is a deeply fulfilling knowledge that lifts our soul above the world reality to a place that gives us true joy and happiness.

The Ostrich Effect

We are facing a social problem of epic proportions. The safety of our ostrich hole will not protect us from the effects of what our current school system is doing to a high percentage of our children. The school your children are attending may not exhibit some of the extreme manifestations we are seeing in some schools. Your child may be coping well with the school system they are in and performing well. The crisis in our school system is like a dam that is leaking. It is hard to determine if the dam will break or just leak forever like dams do, but this dam will break and we will all get wet no matter how well our children are doing in school or how safe we feel now. Doing nothing because you feel unaffected is like playing Russian roulette, what are the chances that the bullet is in the chamber when your child pulls the trigger. Drugs, sex, moral decay, depression, violence, intimidation, and low self esteem; these bullets are heading towards all of us. Parents look at the bigger picture. Be willing to recognize the effects of our school system on other children other than your own. Do you want school to be some kind of intellectual game just because your child is winning? Look past this trap and realize we will all eventually lose with that strategy. Besides, helping all children down the natural path of learning and self-discovery is the right thing to do, your children will benefit as well. With a sincere desire, inspiration and effort (we can overcome anything) all of us can become experts at nurturing our children.

Ingenuity

There are so many brain processes, that we will never understand them all. There are so many brain processes that evolve through the spirit of the individual, not through a school system. School systems will never, no matter how hard they try to manipulate knowledge, be able to take credit for these brain processes' existence. This simple truth should inspire all who read this to abandon our current school system and embrace the natural learning process.

From the Author

I do not know how to express my desire for our society to embrace a school system that does not turn our children into products. My emotions about our life experience runs deep in my soul. When you have felt the oppressing effects of a school system growing up, or when you have watched your beautiful children begin to think they are not smart, something inside your soul cries out.

Words are not going to correct what we are doing to our children; large numbers of concerned people and parents can.

Home-schoolers take their children out to protect them, but this effort does nothing for the millions of children that still go to school. I cannot, in good conscience, based upon what I have observed in my own life, be satisfied with the fact that I have protected my family from our current school system while other families have to endure it.

The fact is, we are all affected our whole lives by how we have educated our children. The challenges we face require that we be honest with ourselves and put the needs of our children first. Home-schooling is not the only answer. We need a public school system, just not the one we have now.

If I could have written a 300-page book on this very important issue, I would have. The fact is, the solution is so simple, few words are necessary.

Field work and new ideas, guided by our sincere desire to do the right thing for our children, is required.

Have you ever used a vise grip to install a bolt? A vice grip, for people who do not know, is a fantastic tool. It is designed to grip something with an enormous amount of pressure. It will install a bolt, but will grind the top of the bolt down making it impossible to use the proper tool on the bolt again. We should never get so hasty to accomplish a task that we use the wrong tool. Let's be patient, let's work through this challenge, and let's start today.

My brain is hard-wired not to inflict my opinions on others. I have considered the possibility that other people do not share my opinion. I have intentionally spared the world over the years from my thought processes.

The desire to write this book became so strong to me, I could not resist it. I hope there are others out there that feel the same way I do. Changes needed to be made in our school system. My ideas and observations are just my ideas; other people might have a lot better ideas. I will be watching and participating in the process, God-willing. If all of our children do not become all that they can be, we will not have succeeded, and we will need to continue the effort until we do.

This manual should be considered fiction by all who read it. Ideas are just that: like science fiction novels. Until someone accomplishes the concept, the concept is just words on paper.

To order more copies of The Intellectual Bondage Of Our Children, cut out this page and fill it out. Mail it to:

Greentimber Schoolhouse
P.O Box 787
Ashton, Idaho 83420

Qty_____ x $18.95 = _____

Ship to my address:
_____
_____
_____
_____
Checks only, no cash or money orders.

Shipping and handling no charge.